REED MU

OTHER POETRY BY PETER LEVI

Collected Poems 1955–1975
Five Ages
Private Ground
The Echoing Green
Shakespeare's Birthday
Goodbye to the Art of Poetry
Shadow and Bone
The Rags of Time

IN TRANSLATION

George Pavlopoulos: The Cellar

PETER LEVI

Reed Music

ANVIL PRESS POETRY

Published in 1997
by Anvil Press Poetry Ltd
Neptune House, 70 Royal Hill, London SE10 8RT

This book is published with financial assistance
from the Arts Council of England

ISBN 0 85646 279 9

A catalogue record for this book is available
from the British Library

Designed by Anvil
Set in Monotype Ehrhardt
Printed and bound in England by
Arc & Throstle Press, Todmorden

FOR DEIRDRE

NOTE

For some years it will be seen I was obsessed with a poem by Valéry, which I had misunderstood, miscounting the stanzas. Still, it remained close to me until last summer after writing about Philip Sherrard I roughly translated it, and print that still unsatisfactory version at the end of this book. I wrote it after Horace and before Virgil. Otherwise the chronology of this collection of poems is not to be trusted.

P.L.

CONTENTS

Reed Music

Autumn and the sky shaking with swans' wings.
The dying summer has a hundred tones:
laborious love-moans of the wind that sings
among wild, withered fruit of whitening bones.

The whole lake is consuming with swanfire:
the surface of green marble, chilly cold,
transmuted when the sun falls, to inspire
mere reed music as the muse loses hold:

Apollo's with the swans, he will return
with the buzz and whirr of them, he will awake
whom now the sun drags with his fainting burn
from the last kiss that lingers in the lake.

Where to Go, What to Do

Black coffee in the early flush of sun
lays out the bookish day until you may
cheat nightfall by the creeping of the pen,
and yellow wine like sun in the cold sea,

who breaks in surf over his shelly sand
punctuating his voice with curlew cries
too wild for the words trailing under your hand,
to end in lost sea-breath and salty sighs.

You cannot trap the rawness of the world
or spell sea-truths out with old orange-skins,
not though you follow all the wind has hurled
a thousand ways, and boil up tea in tins.

Poem for the Time of Year

HOMAGE TO VALÉRY

I

The frizzled grass is dusty, sun has shone,
the lake is still and the last boat is gone:
woods like a bank of cloud darken to coal,
yellow edges of trees hardly awake
let their shadows extend in the green lake,
black diamond, it shivers like the soul.

II

Autumn. Only the children in pure ease
cry out at play among the ruined trees
old willows sigh and mumble like the brain's
green empty tangles haunted by birdsong,
and we walk home, our summer was too long,
and the leaves lie like litter in the lanes.

III

Time carries all away, in one immense
motionless waterfall of innocence,
too slow, too powerful for our knowledge;
lakes, images, skies, we are not like them
or the inspired woods breathing their poem
where lean blackberries gleam in the wild hedge.

IV

All summer the tall yachts like butterflies
flaunted their coloured wing that never dies,
then when the sunset folded it away,
swimming the lake like children of daylight
to lie trembling with tinkling mast all night:
now the claypit lies silent as the clay.

V

The closing petals of the dark enfold
a smell of leaves and water and the cold:
earth-rooted images dissolve in night,
and heaven fills with stars fainting to take
their snap-shots of the surface of the lake;
only the trees live on in a half-light

VI

that lingers brooding like a desert noon
while the long lake has comfort from the moon:
because the flower of the dark will break
open again, and shut petals will fall
in the dawn wind, and watch the dead woods all
paint themselves on the surface of the lake.

VII

Love is night's fool and paints a deeper dark.
The owl is the moon's bird, and the moon's work
is streaks of water-gold and poetry
and low-toned musing of the wandering owl,
night flights, winter paintings, the vixen's howl,
and the long tidal washes of the sea.

VIII

The dying world has cold and peaceful breath,
man dying sooner sees a deeper death,
he has his unbelief, his faith that feeds
where the dark lake looks infinitely deep
in meadows where the wild swans seem asleep
and the wind only whispers in the reeds.

IX

An apple that had reddened on the bough
long polished by the wind has tumbled now
to lie slug-slobbered in the long wet grass,
the wind of autumn rises fresh from rest
and sings out like a pastoral tempest.
The long season of fruits begins to pass.

X

We wake to the cock crying, the goat-bleat,
billowing clouds, the sun and his small heat:
we who dug out the claypits on the heath
and keep these woods and meadows only see
gilded, dark, meagre immortality,
thin comforter with the appalling wreath,

XI

clouded in thunders and the ghastly flare
of heaven's snake-skin glittering in midair:
what can we do but listen for the loud
roar of that storm, that disappearing scene
when stubborn rain lashes the sodden green
and thunder-strokes echo from cloud to cloud?

XII

All that is natural passes like a style,
now autumn has green-gilded what was vile,
cobwebbed corruption with raindrops and sighs,
hung fruit against the yellow leaf, attacked
the mist with colours, suffered death to enact
perpetual transformations of our eyes.

XIII

The equinox brings colder, shorter days
of wind and frost and the thin evening haze,
when lake water shivers at the first breeze,
and fishermen quiet in the last sun
grow cold and leave the water one by one,
dark, clouded crystal of lost images.

XIV

And now the chestnut branches are as bright
yellow as feathers in the lessening light,
the lonely mystery of a birdcall
lures the late sun behind the ruined trees,
and (breath and bones) our last resort is peace,
to watch the apples ripen and then fall.

XV

Spirit of earth still fuming in the dark:
it is the Dionysus of Plutarch
forever dying, forever reborn:
like those thin spirits of the trees that shake
on the wind-worried surface of the lake,
the god in his passion forever torn

XVI

by storms of our unquiet element
by generation, pleasure, discontent,
whose buried self death has disenchanted:
spirit of things that longed in their brief lives
for everlasting stillness and yet strive
towards the resurrection of the dead.

XVII

Fish lorries churn along the Bristol road,
the dying sun and moon that have bestowed
these sombre tones and the decaying thud
in the far woods have passed on to the earth
their gift of life, their talent for rebirth,
their strange colours have ended in the mud.

XVIII

This winter's geese flying in from the sea
mock the pale blue skies of eternity,
and this winter's hedges let loose their hair
white in the wind, the river's sandy head
just rises to roll over in his bed,
vigorous swans swim the blue streams of air.

XIX

The stars sprinkle like salt and it is night,
the summer has burnt out like a flashlight:
it is an element of winter now,
all that green ceremonious ripening
and the sun's honey and the scent of spring
have withered to dead leaf and withering bough.

XX

The sap drops, the tree freezes, the soul shrinks,
and waking in pink dawn the vixen drinks
from the dark circle of the wooded lake,
the skeleton is thirsty in the earth,
impotent to bring itself to rebirth,
the paths are undisturbed that she will take.

XXI

This rustic solitude, the spirit sated
with mere enigmas and the unabated
rush of hill water rustling down the stones:
it flows into the tide, only to be
the neverending ending of the sea
breaking on rock, the earth's unbroken bones.

XXII

Things drown in water meadows at their ease,
Severn mingles her waters in pure peace
with tributary streams chewing the land,
and where the mist lies like an opium dream
reeds hardly stir, and the wet meadows gleam,
she sucks at earth and heaves herself in sand,

XXIII

since all this land is hers and must return
to her where autumn fires now darkly burn:
she hears the hounds of winter and their cries,
drains away cold water from the claypit,
which imagines she has abandoned it
dreaming of dinghies like tall butterflies.

XXIV

Nothing is faithful but the returning sea,
the bitter spray of the sea's ecstasy
and the deep voices of the plunging waves;
all this landscape preparing the sea's bed
is nothing but a cloth the sea has spread
green over woods and cottages and graves.

XXV

Our world is shrinking, day by barren day
the salt wash of the sea will have his way
over house, garden, orchard and beehive
where geese swim and the swallows dip to drink
and where Bristol paints heaven sullen pink,
and where earth licks the scar of the M5.

XXVI

The equinoctial gale reads his long lecture
down avenues empty of architecture:
and the last place of refuge for spirit
is the far coast, the island of the past,
the summer images that will not last,
the world of yesterday that will not fit.

XXVII

Graze on the wind, the swallows are all gone,
now the year's midnight and deathstar comes on.
Graze on the wind that chills away your breath
and on the empty spaces of the sky,
mysterious sign of what it is to die
consumed by the spirit that lives on death.

The Ageing Soul

The soul's flame-tongue mirrors another one,
shivering flesh's hunger is absolute
for the sun, for the sunblast in the sun,
it is not sated with the yellow fruit

that dangles darker now than the fruit-leaf,
springwater is no remedy for thirst,
and the imprisoned soul's hunger for life
will not be nourished where it fed at first.

The cry of the ageing soul is deafening,
at one bird-cry a million birds call
which are not satisfied with anything,
life hungers for fire, fire hungers for all.

As You Were Then

The pale harvest, crows blacker than the trees,
the haze, the yellow blaze in the bare sun:
in childhood you worshipped a field like these,
a landscape riper than another one.

When the lanes ran with darkness like fruit-juice,
of course I love you best as you were then:
war's harvest, big silk horses back in use,
and the stooks tied with straw ties by children.

1942

Pure white, cream yellow of a cricket shirt
at long stop in the afternoon shadow
or where fresh sorrel grew in the long grass,
years stood still, the cricket was so slow.

Of all those names I remember no one
streaming downhill, what pleasure to be free,
like merely running in the lonely woods,
or the dead sun that glittered on the sea.

The Crime

For all these penalties, what was the crime?
Innocent, individual happiness
raining down gently on the naked skin,
and long maturing, gummy essences
rinded in fruit distilled by afternoons,
the apple, crisp and cold and slow as dawn,
the sun drowned upwards into golden light
then the green alterations of all things,
the tree of life withering to knowledge.

Elegy for Miss Benton

Jowett's white cuckoo-owl cried in a dome
which is lost now, Miss Benton was old then,
at Lossiemouth a hundred years ago
Odyssey sang in waves under her keel:
purple and black Aristophanic geese
white-washed the walls of the City of God:
noise of springwater, caverns of jasmine
where Tennyson had bathed his mossy beard.

For Bruce Chatwin

We find ourselves mere pianos of bones,
old, bad poets with swan-encumbered dreams
who have forgotten the sifting of sand
and the fear, morning winds shifting the sand:
troubled by nothing human, only marked
by the wingbeat of virtuous water-birds
by which we came to wells and saving pools
and to the thin fringe of the desert pools
where we have woken now, finding ourselves
water-corrupted, mere pianos of bones
filled with wingbeats of dream-encumbered swans.

Four Pictures of a Poet

I

When blossom first creeps out though leaves refuse
and crystal blazes of short-sighted eyes
clear away ground-mist from the red sunrise
this is bad poetry that I can use;
my skull rings, poetry's the only news,
the silver resonance, the giant size
of the world-theatre where the issue lies
in me: who does not tremble at such views?
But I am shadow, nothing but a voice,
no thought, no nightingale, no night-time trick,
and if the world has mountains I have none:
I do not choose, poems offer no choice,
I do not sing or simulate music,
poetry is all mine, I am no one.

II

The world is flat, and I can roam around
shifting the blue-green jellies of my eyes
to reckon up sunshadow or moon-size
as if I had my feet glued to the ground.
Language is in midair: the words resound
with the faint hiss of water as it dies
or buzzing of a thousand summer flies,
flight of the snow owl, howl of the wolfhound;
poets as men on earth consider these
confusions in the soul float from the edge
of feeling and perception, then grow less
as lark ascending seems a bird at ease,
and echo is thrown back by nothingness
and the crowd shout as horses clear the hedge.

III

The bunch of greenery I wear today
is all I retain from the life I lead,
the freshness lingers like green blood indeed
which dripped down from my sickle yesterday:
summer furrows my face and who can say
whether my poems or the bees I breed
exist for mine or the earth's or the gods' need?
Life is a comedy but not a play.
I turn my eyes to the snow-smitten peaks
where the gods are and winter never melts,
they laze in gold sun where the world began:
well, in this world happy is he that seeks;
I have lived among poets and among Celts,
deluded that I was a happy man.

IV

Cigars enliven me, not cigarettes,
the gross machinery of the picturesque
churns the tobacco-smoke around my desk,
Primavera's content with what she gets
from blinded alleys where the dead sunsets
billow like washing-lines, while Thatcheresque
England goes my way to the true grotesque:
my face is my father's, no doubt obscene
but you'll agree, wonderfully refined,
cosmos reflected as necessity:
because in me there is no might have been,
I have eaten and digested my own mind:
what was, what may be, what it is to be.

On a Garden

Out in the garden in the living world:
perception waited as the garden did
breaking like the sea on the astonished sense,
birds sang a rose opened the bush aspired
the grass drowned old battle-fleets of daisies,
the gardener in this year's bean sticks could hear
neat flapping from a breakfast table-cloth,
tomatoes sprouted and the ants were fed.
Daybreak was the cold iron of handlebars.
You will not find it now on any coast.
It is all in the country of the past.
Whose feet will ever walk in it again?
Were happy in it only yesterday.

In a Monastery Garden (Moscow)

The officers of darkness call for blood,
dismember a dry corpse, dispute a crust
and caw and caw and caw against the sky.
The snow hangs virgin on their battlements
far overtopping the bare twigs of trees
where snow falls as suddenly as sun shines.
All winter's banners break and blow to rags:
the hooded crow glutted with snow-leavings,
bird-brain in thin bird-bone, all but the voice,
spying on spirits like lords in Hamlet
carry bare swords to make nights' bodies bleed.
What will day's fantasies oppose to these
but snowy silent walls, grey roar of wind,
shadows of ruins and the cries of crows?

The Old Village, North Oxfordshire

Bell-roar, elm-muffle, chanting of the cock
parson's voice, squire's accent and doctor's drone
and the sunrise as regular as a clock:
all in the past, and we are left alone;

though we still have a vicar of a kind
and the squire's house is standing but with no park,
and you have to take the early bus to find
a doctor (no weekends, not after dark).

The decline of the parson meant the doctor's rise,
but he lasted the briefest of the three:
who goes to him now for help or advice?
It was sad to see the squire go certainly,

he melted into the roaring of the bells,
and then elm by elm all the trees died,
the cocks are silent, we work somewhere else,
now only the allotments are our pride.

From Verlaine

Music before anything else,
and I prefer the uneven, the odd,
being vague and more soluble in air,
nothing weighs or hangs in it, there's no god.

And you ought not to choose
your words in the hope that doubt will cease,
nothing is nicer than a misty song
in which the undesired links with the precise.

There are fine eyes behind the veils,
there is the big, shivering noon sun,
in the blue sky belonging to autumn
a blue swarm of clear stars shines one by one.

Because we are still seeking the Nuance,
not colour, only nuance, the rest we scorn,
only nuance contrives to marry dream
to dream and the flute to the horn.

Fly further from the murdering point,
cruelty of Spirit, impurity of laughing
which make the eyes of the blue infinite weep
and all this underprivileged cooking.

Take hold of rhetoric and break its neck,
you will do fine with energy, so set
Rhyme in its place as it merits;
with no one watching how far might it get?

Who will recite us all the wrongs of rhyme,
and what deaf child or what maddened negro
confected us this twopenny jewel,
making a noise so false and so hollow?

Music again, and always music!
Let your poem be the something not quite here,
but felt as a soul is felt in full flight
to other heavens and to loves elsewhere.

May your poem be scattered on the wind
as crisp as morning, let it be adventure
smelling of wild mint bushes and of thyme,
and everything else is literature.

Critical Exercise

A poetry whose whim is to repeat
the new against the grain of time, the strange
embodiment of will's unnatural beat
needs eyes as cold as stone to rearrange
its elemental victory as defeat
whose ethos does not change and will not change:

handfuls of flowers gasping in a glass
lean outwards towards life, their thwarted range
brings inwardness like outwardness to pass,
and Mariana in the moated grange
chokes in her allergy to the dead grass
whose ethos does not change and will not change:

the wingbeats of poems define a void
whose dangerous angel can never exchange
those new, impressive gestures which have toyed
with signals that unnerve and disarrange
our antique definitions re-employed
whose ethos does not change and will not change.

Later

Our pleasures have gone over, they have gone
like the plough-horses, where nobody knows,
where the sun went from the poems of Tennyson,
the bird from the dark garden, the crimson rose.

We have lived into formidable years,
the innocent were rejoicing in their beds
but darkness has fallen and they wake in tears,
the dustbins clang, wallpaper hangs in shreds.

Those green mysterious willows on a cream wall
fire blackened and explosions tore apart
have crumbled and revealed nothing at all
but impoverished landscapes, the normal heart.

Retirement

Jeer at the world spinning so fast away
with all its dizzy rhetoric of delight,
just the flare of a spent match at midnight
when the bored shadows hang and hardly play.

We have died or gone back an age in time
down shadowed lanes of willow, the green cream,
the pure vast silver of the river-gleam,
the cuckoo's lonely and perpetual rhyme,

where among woods and pools the aspens lay
their ample waterfalls down like dead breath,
and nothing breathes but happiness and death;
jeer at the world spinning so fast away.

Sins

These old men remembering their sins
and their sins' origin
observing in the craters of the moon
some old explosion some dull afternoon
awake with cries remembering their sins.

Some old men have forgotten their sins
drowned aspirin in gin:
with scarred and happy faces see the sun
as if their youth had just begun,
and smile blessings on one another's sins.

Like a Shadow

You did not hear the shot that hit you
you did not feel the dream that woke you
you did not see the fly that bit you
you don't remember who forsook you.

The fluting birds are not your lovers
they will not go to sleep beside you
and when you sleep the dawn discovers
earth has not anywhere to hide you.

When nothing lies ahead but meadows
you will have stepped into the entrance
like a shadow among the shadows,
then you will understand your sentence.

Time to Move On

These grassy cottages
have black glass where the sun
flares among drowning trees
at dusk, then it is gone,

but nothing marks the days,
little marks any hour,
the distant hills in haze
the sunset water-sour:

the nights are different
and full of quiet rain
or else they are silent,
day is vocal again:

cuckoo wears himself out,
it is a kind of life
untrammeled and untaught
just medicined with grief.

The Remedy

When memory like frost has icy teeth
and the snow drizzles unable to speak,
when love looks unfamiliar like death,
or falling suns drop silver on the lake
burning away the gold they were made of,
then whisky is no remedy for love.

When love invites and the door swings open
small birds are lively and the world is wide,
and the sea that had died revives again
in foams of white painting on the seaside,
love on the rocks broods like an anchorite
and learning is no remedy for it.

When the blackbird scolds in the yellow leaf
and still the lichen-crusted statues sigh
for her who has dissolved into pure grief,
when the heart hums with happiness gone by
and his dusk weakens and his stars are dim,
then music is no remedy for him.

Hotels

Idéal Séjour, Hôtel du Dream:
my friend was happy, someone else was not;
who is happy? I ask in the lush grass,
and the sky-lark still lyrically calls.
In the fields there were shocks and thunderings,
shield and trumpet streaming silver and gold:
fresh leopard, antique lion would engage
melting hot breath, the one colour is mud
spattered with blood, old as metal and cold.
The fine dream of hotels in future time
was not revealed, but still and still I heard
dappled horses and fresher than the dream
randy on dry hay and fresh meadow grass
thundering in the backroom of the skull.
It has rained on the flowers in the field,
there springs up simply an old journalist
out of my breast of bird-infested turf.
This poem has no end, we have no end,
all our life is bound up with any life:
or in some quiet woods a good hotel
where the lark trills on the untried meadow.

The Welsh Marches

Eight linked topographic sonnets
for drawings by Alan Powers

I LANCAUT

Our history ran out into the sand,
my muse and goddess is topography,
the clear Britannia I can understand:
a leaden statue in an icy sea.
A ruined chapel in a green loop of land
musty with grasses and stone mystery:
Lancaut: the painter holds it in his hand,
what we have once been and will never be:
what has scarcely survived, scarcely England,
where Wales pours down a river to run free
on English meadows, eat the sodden land
and murmur and remurmur endlessly,
neither in English nor in Welsh: the bone
of landscape is the shaving of the stone.

II CAPEL Y FFIN

In memory of David Jones, René Hague and Reynolds Stone

The landscape is the shaving of the stone
by the wind, by the rain, the grass on it
shaved with the scythe, sheep-cropped, the hill alone
survives the steel and the steel tongue of wit,
unspoiled and unexhausted and its own.
Suns dive into their west and bit by bit
the Black Mountain calls for another tone,
whose shadows swallow lamps that had been lit
in valleys where there was no telephone
(pure art was clinging there like a limpet).
Freshness then, now the long, secular moon
landscape betrayed, the whisper from the pit:
and yet something clings to the hill, and we
drink hill water in pure sobriety.

III LANDSCAPE (NEAR LORD HEREFORD'S KNOB)

Mountain water and pure sobriety:
from great hill to small hillside it runs down,
vague misty mountainous infinity
down to a valley and a river town:
a thousand yards high is the most you see,
two knobs of charcoal outcrop mildly frown
on slopes of pastoral solemnity:
no verb only a place-name for a noun.
The hills descend to kiss the level sea
like the green flounces of a falling gown
unsettled from the hip, slid from the knee,
to where trout swim in clear and rustic brown,
a view so wanton and so innocent,
out of the sight of God and his judgement.

IV SHOBDON

Out of the sight of God and his judgement
on Shobdon's Gothic stage the risen sun
gleams through the dead men's glass: God is content
to stream like light among us while no one
misunderstands his gentleman's accent.
In all the small hills there is no work done
but by severe seasons or with head bent,
as a bird sings, for small reward or none,
our gospel in our life's re-enactment,
our dying souls as saintly as a nun
flitter moth-like around fine ornament
like an expiring hour-glass whose sands run
slowly away till with the dying light
the season passes and the bone is white.

V MONTGOMERY

The season passes and the bone is white,
lives on as architecture, a new age,
the spirit is consumed, painted up bright,
a town in its beauty like a village:
the simple rows of buildings swim in light:
wisdom was born, blood thrived here and the sage
Herbert of Cherbury took his swan-flight
above these roofs, and the fresh-smelling page
that swan muses had smoothed white to invite
George Herbert, opened in his pupillage:
sons of one mother, whose tongue told the height
of heaven and made milder heaven's rage:
small market town whose pride might only be
the old luxuriance of privacy.

VI POWYS CASTLE

The old luxuriance of privacy
cascades down terraces of openness
from well-made towers: Shakespeare's century
in which the playing never ends, careless
that life at best is a sad comedy:
old houses have bad stories and must bless
our kind of open-ended history:
no God, few drumbeats, no real distress.
The garden has a certain poise, you see
lawn above ordered lawn and you can guess
what sculptor made the leaden statuary:
the house crowns all, the collections are a mess.
Here's a lead figure staring at its own
waterdrip running slowly down the stone.

VII CHERK

Waterdrip running slowly down cut stone
makes an autumnal colour, waterfall
dripped from an aqueduct, the slow motion
that falls and does not fall: the still canal
glides on arches that stride on and on,
and grope from earth high as a Chinese wall
out of this incoherent growth, green tone
and thin bodies of trees where a bird-call
summons up sunset and the feel of bone:
and under these arches our suns will fall
into their west, till the star-skeleton
of human meaning peers down over all.
Beside the slow canal young arches wait
to carry steam-trains and to bear their weight.

VIII FLINT CASTLE

To carry steam-trains and to bear their weight
New England hewed its old chestnut forest:
the road extends, not magnifies the state:
we wallow like cattle in interest.
Who stood guard at Flint Castle? It is late
to ask what greeds or fantasies infest
such dry, clean ruins as still meditate
the spread of dead Empire into the west:
our glory is not severed from our fate,
for the dishonoured, dishonour is best,
the ghost of glory swings with a dead weight
in bizarre ways, but then it comes to rest
where the King's wound looks fresh and bleeding, and
our history ran out into the sand.

Indian Summer

I

The hammer striking with a hollow sound:
someone driving a spike into the ground,
the sun is up, the air empty and clean,
they are tethering a chestnut and white horse
in fresh grass like a pensioned-off racecourse
under the trees, somewhere far down the green.

II

How cold the sun is in the morning now:
the empty green is one mess of shadow
and the leaf sickens on the chestnut trees,
in the evenings a few children appear
and climb in the same branches year by year,
time is still and the sun seems to freeze.

III

The groundfrost vanishes and the clear sky
of melting mist that sees the hills go by
lives only by the movement of the scene,
all down the laneside every feathered throat
that bravely whistles out his autumn note
lives for this day and knows no other one.

IV

But we old men sniff winter in today
and the dampness of night dripping away,
we snuffle older breezes in this breeze,
and fainter flower-smells, a distant noise
stiller than stillness now, of village boys
bicycling in the shadows of the trees,

V

half a life-time ago, so long ago
they are stranded from the soul's ebb and flow
safe from the world's autumnal dying tone:
though the moon swoons on like a cotton kite
they come alive in the fresh waning light,
where soul must recollect itself alone.

VI

The mind plays in the shallows of the soul
or pours itself like soup in a soup-bowl,
but is elusive as a steaming breath,
soul is a canvas Christ, a shadow-king
half in love, half in fear of everything,
a knob of butter that will melt to death.

VII

Old thoughts, old jokes, phrases that we half mean:
it is time now to walk across the green,
the aeroplanes are tumbling in midair
as if this year were nineteen forty-one
and fifty years of struggle all undone,
hot air balloons float by like our despair.

VIII

The bonfires and the cobwebs are the same,
ponies at grass, the children at their game:
the silent turn of season that achieves
stubble and wheatstraw, wild fruit in the hedge,
trees loaded, the field trampled at the edge,
and the slow colours changing on the leaves.

IX

The stillness in the air summons me up,
and the dry acorn rolling from his cup
in the long grass does not trouble the calm,
a morning cobweb trembles in the light
and a tree transfigured to his full height
lurches with his own shadow arm in arm.

X

Time does not move although I hear it chime,
mere self-intoxication of the time
freezes the earth for one moment so still
black water does not move, a feather floats,
and swans without passion rest their white throats
and the sun hangs silent over the hill.

XI

It is a hoarded after-taste of life,
sun blasting the sun-eaten chestnut leaf,
sun-dazzle down the green along the pond,
sun smoking in a bare heaven that rings
with the near silent whizzing of swan wings
and the geese muttering on the lake beyond.

XII

The wind gets up, the world goes sliding round
from hope to hope, the sun sinks underground,
and the last children quit the lonely grass:
children's children, still shouting at their play,
the riders and the dogs desert the day,
it is the equinox, the wind will pass.

XIII

The equinoctial gales blow themselves out
and the cold mind goes tilting into doubt,
the balance of the year tilts from a mark
which cannot be recovered any more;
while we wet our cold hands on the cold shore
of our side of the earth, the sea is dark.

XIV

Yet after such a dark, such a morning
of melancholy light as bright as spring,
as rich in colours, as subtly perfumed:
and sober wind to thresh the autumnal trees,
riot of the senses humming like bees
and soul in the soul's darkness self-consumed.

XV

It is the afterseason of old men
and of the faithful hearts in love with them,
their limbs look deathly and their heads are bare,
they feed birds on the green with breakfast crumbs
as they scattered their life, and that becomes
honey distilled from trees into the air.

XVI

One bird whistles and the field-fruit is ripe,
memory is confused into a heap
and everything in nature seeks for rest:
birds in the hedges, berries in the bush,
the vixen howling in the nightfall hush:
I had not thought life's ending was this feast.

XVII

Old men wander through the grey afternoon
over rough grass as the dewfall comes on
at one with birdflight threading through midair
and fugues of jackdaws in the ragged trees:
old men take time to notice things like these
and minutes to get up out of a chair.

XVIII

The field thistle should be their flower-crown
dim purple and crude green and thistle-down.
Only the oak tree draws the thundercrash,
crop a thistle, she flourishes again,
storm moves inshore swinging a tail of rain,
the steady scything of the lightning flash

XIX

does not disturb the thistle where she grows
on unploughed ground or old river-meadows:
these old men are confused, their thoughts ash-light,
whatever the day's weather says to them
the vigour of the thistle's in the stem,
thistle-down's off away to any height.

XX

And I grieve for these old men at their ease
and for the gilded bronze wreath on the trees
and the dead water round the rotted oak:
sign after sign and then one handsome sign:
between the crooked trees a laundry line
billowing like the sun on cannon-smoke.

XXI

Trees may drip honey though the bees have gone,
sunlight distils away, the trees drip on,
of all the year's grass this is the greenest
caught by one finger of the falling sun,
trees look immortal now, sheep need no one,
Severn hatches the islands of the blest.

XXII

The light draws inward into old men's eyes,
I think soul is a tissue of goodbyes,
the cock at dawn crowing in the ground-mist
and the dawn shivering on a bed of dark
woke ghostly trees stalking across their park,
where the stars scarcely glimmer or exist.

XXIII

Age peers easily out at the sun's ray
and as the tanned skin feels the glow of day
knows life is embers, blows, and kindles it.
They know winter is coming, they have seen
the dying year sweeping across the green,
the cattle stabled, and the bonfires lit.

XXIV

But now who can recall the forest sigh,
the cuckoo's melancholy stony cry?
The Shadowman has tangled up the ground,
and though the mist echoes we only hear
the sourest hunting-horn die in the ear
and the hoof striking with a hollow sound.

Poem for the Time of Day (Gillan Creek)

I

The silence of the earth is for the weak,
the green water that slides along the creek
consumes the heron rusting silently:
seasons and afternoons will not be long
and the bell sounds only for evensong
in hanging woods that tremble tree by tree.

II

Death is no weaker and no more silent
than I am now, I am ashes, content
to watch the motions of the glittering tide
like silver paper crinkling into light
where the green surface broadens out of sight
and the mist burns and quiet dinghies ride.

III

It is a restoration after all
of old sand-haunting figures you might call
defeated by the world and by our lives,
when the ghost in the body is set free
by the decay and freshness of the sea
and by sea-light honing itself like knives.

IV

The rolling clouds as slow as seasons pass
and the sun withers to a voice of grass,
I am left lonely with song-birds that trail
from month to month, or sing and are not seen
in the great field of blue and dazzling green,
the curlew, then the lonely nightingale.

V

The woods hang silent high above the creek,
two walls of falling waves that never break,
there the young nightingale tunes her soft throat
hidden among wild roses, clear as gin,
annihilating human sorrow in
a labyrinth of greenness, note by note.

VI

The broken pebble loves the water-lick:
I am old, I am comforted by rhetoric,
even the rhetoric of an invisible thing
which utters what the salt floodwater is
and the soul's hunger for adversities
and the woods melting when the muses sing.

VII

A wind attacks the blue blossom of day
and the broad water wrinkles in the bay,
how glass-coloured the sea is, and how cold,
how tremulous now in the morning breeze
under the shadows of the cloudy trees,
how hard when the sun touches it with gold.

VIII

The boats at anchor sway from side to side
as they nod in the tugging of the tide,
they are gripped in the long pull of the sea
as lightly held as the tall sailing suns
running their course in heaven as the sun runs
above your tideless depth, eternity.

IX

Small flowers in the sand of the seashore
flourish colours that there is no name for,
purple or white or a sea-faded red
in the thin grass under the lightest leaf,
like memories reviving, pure as grief,
and the sea has his dirges like the dead.

X

Always beginning, always again, the sea
drowns his own dirges in what is to be,
greenness and foam crowding inshore to die
like falling walls in tawny clouds of sand,
till the sea lies at full length on the land:
immortal vigour, infinite as the sky!

XI

The long creek does not look so very long,
tamed by owl-hoots, heron-cries, curlew-song,
and soft exploding rooks in the dead trees
that stand around the tower: sea-water creeps
along a mile of rocky nest, and sleeps
where the gull mews and the weed floats at ease.

XII

Above the headland rocks and old sea-scars
a single night-bird chants under the stars:
self-loving music midnight has set free,
and yet the night-chant is not what I love,
since I am old I value little above
the self-delighting descant of the sea.

XIII

It is the sea making love with the earth,
so barren they will bring nothing to birth,
the sea's cold breath dissolving as it flies,
the sea's immense blue shoulder and rough head,
the sea's mouth crushing the earth's lips to sand,
with kisses and mere swigs and briny sighs.

XIV

How odd to think that all this might have been
Virgil transformed into a water-scene:
squalor of mud and weed and bone-white shells
transmuted to a glimmer in the sea
while the wave goes and comes so patiently
disguising time: yet it is time that tells,

XV

and the still creek-water in quiet motion
mimics the falls and heaving of the ocean:
the sea alive, alive, and still the same
far away out of sight, cape beyond cape,
clouded mirror pregnant with light and shape,
house of life flickering upwards like a flame.

XVI

Bone whitens and lies still on the sea-bed,
sea-transformations, voices of the dead,
unresting idleness, tranquillity
in the dark apparatus of the waves,
the dying sun that drowns, the dawn that saves,
the potency and purple of the sea,

XVII

alive in mind one unextinguished same,
like the dim yellow of a candle-flame:
as if the moon's mirror could pause in flight
over sea-pools older than all the ages
and ringed round with deliberate images,
and swarms of stars that settled at tree-height.

XVIII

Flower and star and leaf wither and pass
to darkness with hog-parsley and goose-grass
and the sun's draggle is a long goodbye,
the summer's weather, these mountains of cloud
and the song-thrush of dawn that was so loud
and the blue patches of the vivid sky.

XIX

The soul is feeble, it lies down beside
the unresisting languor of the tide
and seems to die because it burns so low,
runs out in seas, is lost, is shadow-thin,
the soul's weight is a cypher ending in
a slate tablet, and Here lies So-and-so.

XX

Listen: the tide: ocean inexorable
banging the water-doors of his green stable,
but the sea-horses fling their white foam back
galloping loose through light and through half-light,
barren as the spirit they give delight
breathing freedom and death, and leave no track

XXI

because the sea is hungry and spirit
breaks loose and then sighs back to rest in it:
and there is nothing that these waters seek
when the gale sweeps them and the Atlantic rain
lashes them and the moon is horned again,
but to lie quiet in the swelling creek.

XXII

When the storm thins out and the tide recedes
and life glitters in the gleaming of weeds,
day will break open, waves be cold and crisp
and ocean summon from his bluest deep
transfigurations murmuring in their sleep,
in their plashing and splashing lapse and lisp.

XXIII

The sun trundles across heaven alone
like a dumb signal made of fire and bone,
but the entire sea speaks praises to it,
and the creek glitters with mysterious rock,
deep green, damp fire, then where the dinghies rock
it trembles in mere tongues of fire, spirit

XXIV

that moves over the surface of the sea,
far out, far off, and there mysteriously
echoes the heavens and the light they leak
cascading down a million shades of green,
the wood-silence, the sea-whispers between,
and the still heron idle in his creek.

Professors

I shuffle my regrets like playing-cards,
much haunted by the ghost of old men's voices,
their gestures and their faces work in me,
yet of their speech I can recall no word,
they are kings in the underworld of dream:
collegiate buzz of a tenor honey-bee
heard in cloisters and lost long ago
beyond Wye, on the bare high hillside:
an old bee-drone in a meadow of pink clover,
learning dripping like honey from a spoon
out of the stone mouth of an antique mask:
and that wild swarm, soul of antiquity,
those passionate Germanic organ-notes
only the god set free, death ended them:
and now that I have come to the cool dark
I find my voice is weaker than a bee's.

Survival

The days run on and there are so few left,
and the black poplar groans at the park gate.
And there goes half the morning dreamed away.
Thin ghost in a tall chair lapping coffee,
watch till dawn's early intensities
wash away with the hoarfrost from the field
and mist burns away from the still canal.
Glue your nose to the orange in fresh leaf
sunbathing on the bathroom window sill
while the air shakes with the wingbeat of swans;
we will live to see wall-roses again
on cottages quiet as an island.

Forgetfulness

Suddenly one day late in summer
sun races among shadows on the green
and I have washed my eyes awake in it.
Why have I forgotten Walt Whitman?
The sun's psalm climbs among cloud clusters
and cumulus crumbles in the quiet west;
poems have slipped away in sleep half written,
the mind cries out from ninety parts of sleep:
a bird voice falls as lightly as a leaf falls,
and the surf-fall sparkles in green shadows.

For Alan Hancox

One might imagine tendrils of Elgar
among the stucco and stone of Cheltenham.
Music, and what was printed clear and fine,
things bypassed on the margin of our time,
and now our time has settled down to make
old pacifism glow with virtuous health:
and the day primrose-dappled as it dawned
and grey and primrose smudges at sunset.
This young man being nobody frequented
an empty field somewhere high on Cleeve Hill,
where he would see Paul Nash recording trees,
combing skies geometric at sunrise
or brushing stiffness from the earth and trees.
The coldness and the fineness of that air
made it seem aeroplanes could live forever,
while the Queen ripened and the state withered.
These things have not fallen as we supposed.
Used to come to this village: he recalled
a mile of empty green where horses grazed,
and often overheard a whirr of swans.
A shilling bought a big grey ammonite
from boys who got them in the Severn mud
between the sedges where the tide ran out,
while grassy Severn heaved and trickled there.
Northward the queer shapes of the Malvern hills
impertinently showed their silhouettes.

*

Brave, ashen-faced old bookseller and friend,
whose shop was dark and like a mind at peace,
lived in, full of surprises, unfinished;
down there we talked the afternoons away,

death was our subject, and we welcomed it,
but looking back I see nothing but life.
Long fingers stroked an early Tennyson
and your eyes glinted at the Four Quartets,
thin pamphlets printed first in our young days.
We have lived our life to the far edge:
it was not like a walk across a field,
the ragged shadows and the shy birdsong
are colder than the coldness of the world.

Convalescence

I lay and listened for the fruit to fall
while the sea wind tore at the tousled trees
till sea fret muffled up the heron's call
and crows cried their bleak descant to the sea's
soft banging like a bell.

I am caught in poetry's repeated breath,
in Irish poet and Russian novelist
old travellers trawling for their own death:
torn so between rank sunset and fresh east
I must rise like a wraith

in common words and the sun's ragged fires
held frozen by the cold venus of the moon,
my song the wet curlew's that nothing tires:
tang of rain hammering the window-pane
where the sea-wave expires.

I am haunted by no images but these:
green Cornish water, the sun's dying life
left over where the season swam at ease
in scale-armour of sun-dress, and the bright knife
of stars dripped with surprise.

Question

The fruit trees are ready and they undress,
apples drop all around and the grass sings
and the wasp flickering like a candle-flame
stumbles in sun among the windfall pears,
till the day turns to weeping and decline.
Mute rainfall tugs at the hat-brim of the ghost
who will track me unless I pin him down
with the true question, the last question:
then our long conversation can begin.
The high tide of the whole year comes heaving in
to jot his pencil truths on the cloud-bank;
there is no mark left on the bleak foreshore.
The fruit trees and the willow trees undress.

Defeat

Lucid honey of dawn, the rooks in voice
all autumn to the long smear of sunset:
and the scythe reaps and weeps, we pay the price,
nightsweat and day's defeat:

the sum of the soul now is fallen leaves,
the lost, wind-tattered voices of the rooks,
hedges as quiet as winter bee-hives,
dim sheep-eyes, dying looks.

Yet in this mood we could learn to love life,
a stony shell of moon melting away
muffled in clouds like Orpheus in his grief
kissing Eurydice.

Morning Dreams

So many suns have been dissolved in sleep:
and there were the white stars of dawn that creep
hissing up from the bay,
the moon melts into day:

snow-woman gone to moisture in bare sky,
and casual scarves of flame or cloud may fly
on errands of the light:
I belong to the night,

and live now in half-sleep and morning dreams
reading the dark until mere twilight seems
the most life had to show,
and will reclaim me now.

For Easter (1995)

Before the freezing water of the moon
with virgin hands broke open the fresh stone
that was the world's and air's and water's shrine,
the darkness knew and the darkness alone
the death-blood running cold, the murdered man
who was murdered before the world began,
and the still water murmured on the bone
and the blood trickled cold onto his stone,
and gross darkness attended on him then,
who rose up in the darkness and has gone.
Not blood but living water runs again
out of the broken rock where he lay down,
he has trodden on the darkness like a sun,
like the first sun that ever rose and shone.
Who lay dead for the long nights that have gone
and through the seventh day that has undone
the working elements of our creation:
death was the garden that he wandered in,
his own death wound that flowered there so fine,
and his death was the stone he rested on:
for six days he suffered under the sun,
the death of God and his rest make seven:
now it is all finished and he has gone,
he has broken open the unhandled stone,
only spirits and the grave-clothes remain,
the darkness knows when, and the dark alone,
and the dumb kingdom he has made his own
who is the world's and air's and water's shrine.
I believe in the Christ who has risen,
who lay down in his death and now is gone.
What was my morning is my afternoon
and sixty years and more drench my head in
the ashes of my own and Adam's sin,

but I am washed as white as a clean bone
and shall arise out of my death and shine
and be revived and go where he has gone,
whose resurrection takes another tone
with life and time, and all things they feed on:
it is another age that has begun,
and this is a new earth, where new suns shine,
there was no antique sun that ever shone
with this light, but the waning of the moon
that was the world's and air's and water's shrine
leads only down into an age like mine.
I believe in the blood and in the stone
and the innocent one who is one alone.

N. G.

A poem lived: a bottle in the shade:
the music played, the old artist is dead
I am afraid, and I can hear him wade
through shallow water where the stream is wide.

Voyage

An old ship's engine churns up sea and time
with an indignant outcry of sea-birds
crying who suffers and how long a time:
prisoner at the bar, prisoner of snow-white birds;

they are spray-cleaned and sun-polished in flight
while we in our dark-painted water-plough
summon up stars and their unfurrowed flight
and imitate the nothing that they plough,

till dawn brings back the prophecies of birds
and our pretention falls away in time,
dies away in the cries of hungry birds:
the engine churns a furrow dark as time.

Today I saw an island caught in flight
grape-coloured, half-transparent, charcoal grey
at sunrise, lemon-smelling at midnight,
we have not turned, it vanished into grey.

Sir Harry Vane, and Postscript

5 SONNETS

I

I see the water hesitate and hang
back for a moment, and the swan melting,
fresh in black water while the bronze men ring
limb by chopped limb in disarticulate song
to be consumed in cannon for the king,
and the bronze men come tumbling down who rang
trumpet-toned at their first awakening,
whose play now is bell-song, to sing ding-dong;
where did the cannon of the king go wrong,
that thunderous gun-mouth, the bell-blasting
that ruined walls, the sizzle and the sting?
It is the undercurrent that is strong,
and the white lightning of the burning wing
in fields where bronze men stood and bells give tongue.

II

Now it is time to bring back iron men,
dead men who dabbled in those bloody dawns
before the axes hacked them and brought down
their good old cause that never rose again
or slowly rose, black smoke, a burning town,
cracked bones and the mocked ashes of dead men,
the stink and fuming of the fatal crown.
It is time now for men like Harry Vane
a twenty-four years old American
who sniffed the republic in the air of Maine
and felt it in him, servant of the king
trading in woods with the free Indian,
then Cromwell's minister; Milton in hiding
heard he died better than most Englishmen.

III

The decade crumbles and the ashes cool
to candy colours like a barber's pole
while a blind fiddler out of Lear, the fool
has howled his heart out, mile by country mile,
he does not know what influences steal
down from the shelly moon around his soul,
the crust he sucks is dunked in the cow-pool
and the time he plays out is damnable:
his bone-marrow is starkly musical,
rainclouds hiss down like family to reveal
his innermost music, and worst of all
in crumbling rain, in withering dewfall,
worst when decades crumble, when ashes cool,
his dancing time which is the world's downfall.

IV

Long dusty tail of time that has no end:
it tyrannizes only in the mind
and yet stardust is still as many-toned
pure golden frost-white, silver newly cleaned,
exploding fireworks that might scorch your hand
as fresh as sea-spray tingling in the wind:
I see the gods in sea and air and ground
who were so animally warm and blind
no longer trouble or concern mankind,
they used to lurk at tree-height to descend
and find a friend, but are not to be found
because the dusty tail of time is lined
with volume on volume, all well reasoned
long windings of our past, our idiot kind.

V

I would not bring back nineteen thirty-nine
but deep grass and shadows, nineteen fourteen:
straws swam in the lane from waggons then,
the young wasp came blazing from the bright sun
and the cobweb blew all day long alone:
the beards of barley bristle like dead men
and the marine muttering when the moon shone
once heard on Mainalon, mad and divine,
made oxen like gods, gods like horned oxen
and the Rhine water flooded deep and green
a coin glittered deep down, the air so fine
that you can watch the mulberries blacken,
and the year is always nineteen fourteen:
and you will not see nineteen thirty-nine.

The Ghost of Roses

At twenty-one in the night serenade
Mozart was gentle as the summer died:
and in their second flower, then their third,
the oldest, latest roses have faded,
the dog flops half asleep from shade to shade
and the leaf yellows and a cooler tide
runs in under the trees, and shadows ride
where lazy summer's ditches hardly flowed,
but while the sun was in his burning pride
with our burnt bodies wasted, and afraid
that rain might never fall until we died,
night after night all summer I have layed
in the bed of Cleopatra, where there sighed
the ghost of roses sleeping by my side.

Night Visions

The sea is full of shadows, I am free
diving like phosphorus out of the sun
grow darker than the shadows in the sea,
and the fish, black and silver in the moon,
whose small, high voices carry plaintively
flit like the ghost of leaves when autumn's gone,
shadow of a shadow, long dark body
like lovers yearning for another one.
A minute of it is enough for me,
I must come up to breathe where the waves run
mingling in one another, and I see
night visions that the daylight has undone,
the glimmer of the whale's bulk and the sigh
with which he spouts starlight into the sky.

Dream City

I dreamed a dream city when morning was breaking
        more lovely than true,
that the spires and the domes of the city of Oxford
        were painted bright blue:

sky-colour, no joke and too milky for Cambridge,
        new-created and good,
lots of space and no traffic, and there in the middle
        the library stood:

as bright as the sun on a leaf that the May wind refreshes
        right down to the root,
or as if all the lead and the stone had that moment arisen
        at the sound of the flute.

I have dreamed in my time of far heavier cities and rivers
        more broad than young Thames,
where the curtains of brick drip and crumble, the smoke and
                the ruins
        and the city in flames.

Turning-Point

It is these darker mornings taught the Muse
to attend upon Milton blind in his bed,
day after day, no birds' song to confuse
that chanted, tranquil watersong of the dead.

Woods sicken and the leaf falls away fast,
the earth is cold with ground-mist and moon-haze
and now the equinoctial gales have passed
and towards morning one bright star will blaze.

Like a Folk-Tale

When we were born in 1931,
we grew so slowly and so easily,
summers so casual and breath so free
innocent animals under the sun
before life had begun,

we opened our young self like a box of toys
without wisdom but no doubt gratefully,
you were a dream tangled in leaves to me,
I was a horse to you, a sunlit poise
dissolving in hoof-noise.

In 1945 we were fourteen,
we thought the wars were over, victory
like a game, irony by irony
revealed a life that no one had foreseen,
and veiled what it might mean.

So many years, so many tears ago,
washed up together by the blind salt sea
like a folk-tale. I loved you and you me:
nothing to give you but a kiss, and so
let's kiss, the sun is low.

Ghost of an Old Curse

In Houndsditch an old man I never saw
came round Turkish and Jewish warehouses
selling halva, pistachio nuts, loukoum,
and had done since the nineteenth century.
Where is he now, and where is his son now?
Who, from what pool had plaited the straw bags,
reedstraw like ribbon for the fishmonger?
Who worked at the sign of the button-hole maker?
Or found a snake asleep in a rolled carpet
never unrolled maybe since Isfahan?
My God, I think the ghost of an old curse
still hangs above us like the plague of flies,
and the whole of our race is perishing.
By what green water did the reeds grow ever
flattened and plaited to the yellow bags
to take home half a salmon from Scotland,
and half of Euston station stank of fish?
We have perished, and still the cloud is black.

On a Photograph of Highnam Mummers

The beetles trundle onwards with their lights
far down the green into the sleet and snow.
The year slides backward into winter
and a chaos obliterates the stars.
My eyes are bad, and yesterday I fell
but falling caught the dog in weak torchlight,
now the oven's ice-cold, and the long night
sets in. At Christmas in 1918
The Highnam Mummers snug in new whiskers
dressed in dead men's cavalry uniforms
with cutlasses for scimitars had not
cut back the brambles of the wartime woods.

Epitaph

They kissed and then they crept
into the earth and slept.

In sua voluntate e nostra pace

PARADISO III: 85–102

Our entire peace lies quiet in his will:
that is the sea to which all things descend
which he creates, and all natures fulfil.
Now it came clear all places without end
in heaven are paradise, and yet the grace
of the supreme good falls quite unconfined:
like being satisfied with some one taste
yet to be hungry for another one,
to ask for this, leave that with a cheered face;
and so by word and act spoken and done
I sought what the web was she had not drawn
through to the end, although the thread was spun.
'Perfect life and high merit of her own
put this lady so high in heaven,' she said,
'for by her rule the veils are sewn and worn
by those who sleep or wake till they are dead
with that lover who will accept all vows
charity made and his love dictated.'

H. S. L.

With the war over, with the day over,
he read the evening paper in the garden room
aiming glass eyes at the sun of suburbs
till cineraria flowered deeper blue,
and who knows what became of the children?
Somewhere in autumn's air a bucket-clang,
the hands of water will transform a stone:
while the blood-fish rioting like dolphins
leapt with the breaking of a wave in sand,
to sleep in rotted foliage of veins.
Time leaves no trace on the long afternoon,
time is electric, the clock is silent.
An elm tree grieving in his shabby field.

For Angus MacIntyre

D. 21 DEC. 1994

I

The New Building, still haunted by the shade
of William Yeats, great poet and great goof
searching for Elementals on the roof:
a lighted match that flares up, and is dead:

while Sibthorpe's plane tree stretches in the dark
boughs that had stiffened all the afternoon:
they toss and chase under a stony moon
to where the small deer huddle across the park.

Or it is raining, the tree's age and pain
wash away into night, a kind of moan
shivers the leaves, and autumn is quite gone,
the tree sleeps in the stillness of the rain.

II

The boys are playing cricket down the green,
it makes a pause in football, that long game
that begins in September in the mist
after dawn, but before the horses wake,
when stars drown and the dog-fox owns the green,
to end in May, the village's season,
like Ireland or two hundred years ago:
we will not last, football will swallow all,
cricket needs the sewn ball the crack-willow
that the old women brewed up into tea,
it needs the wicket and the willow bat,
football is coarser, they play all day long:
soon after school ground-mist covers the grass,

still they play on, cricket is in the grave,
long after the dark falls you can hear them.
And all our old pleasures appear ghostly,
loose horses in the field phantom horses,
I hear the spirit of a coughing ewe,
the love-struck vixen barking in the night
as she barked on the edge of villages
in Ireland or two hundred years ago.

III

I will wake Izaak Walton from his book
to summer in Scotland, the dripping moon:
up on the mountain, water from the spring
so clean it gives a pure taste to whisky,
and where the stag will turn his noble head
downhill, trotting across the rutted ride
to hear the rattle of the climbing car
with children on the bonnet as it climbs.
Far from here now, and deeper among the trees
Angus, I see you casting for trout
greyest of shadows in dark stream-shadows
brightest of brown, red-spotted, slimed with light.
And now *I wish for some somniferous*
potion to waste my days until that time:
I will walk the fields beside some gliding stream
to enact the quietness of that lost time.
But where is the ground now where *the dew-worm*
will rise to a walnut leaf steeped in water,
in what ditch does the winter minnow lurk
on whom the trout will pounce as a hawk pounces,
where is the woman who could sew a minnow
with *sad French silk, and pale green and white silk*
and silver threads and the black beaded eyes,
that could enchant a trout in fast water

where all is glitter, all glittering shadows?
In the estuary, where the sea-trout run,
I see you like a rock for quietness,
or human heron, born to riversides,
fishing the black pool in your antique hat.

IV

To count intelligence by funniness,
sparkle in the eye, spring in the footstep,
look for the lurching of the coming friend,
or to think all prizes were God-given
and fell by nature to one's dearest friends,
was a mistake of course, easy to make.
Hungary was blackness, then Suez
the long-playing comedy of our summer:
of all Oxford you were the only one
recalled to the Brigade. Governments fell,
the regiment to Cyprus, luggage to Malta,
and generals Gods knows where. 'We shall drive again
to Ghiza up that avenue of palm-trees,
when the cocktails are clinking at the polo-ground.'
And when at last your trunk came back to Hertford,
there on the top was a cummerbund.
Now suddenly it does seem long ago:
time has forgotten us, does Jesus College
groan to itself, forgetting Dom Moraes,
or Hertford grieve to itself over Pingrams
self-murdered, and the mountain where he fell?
We old men see life as a casual river,
where the grey salmon quiver in the stream
keep rank and order, like shadows
as we look down from the stone parapet.
Will there be bridges in the world to come?
And it is years now since I saw the stars,

my youth is like the inferno of Dante
where men are motionless, but the fire moves:
youth is too far to be revisited,
yet in you it was always still alive,
the sparkling fire grew deeper in your eyes
as you grew wiser than an owl in Lear,
snow-owl of midwinter, when the snow lies,
and of all men, of all teachers, all friends,
the most hospitable, most compassionate
and the most liberal I ever knew.
I hear you reassure me about wars,
because almost all soldiers who serve in wars
do it against their will, so very badly:
I hear your comfort over ancient Britain
because in the end, swine as the Romans were,
the British did give them such a bad time.
One night we dined together in your college
where landscapes flourished in sepulchral dark,
and it occurred to me my dear old friend,
that you are all O'Connell liberated.

V

There is a wildness in the eyes of youth
that terrifies me now though I nourished it,
there is a wildness in the eyes of age
savage as eagle's eyes, prophetic, mad
and full of rage to bring down fire from heaven
and leave this island cinders in the fog
that now is green and the grey seal visits
and the big sea-otters swim in the loch.
There is a wildness hidden like humour
fed from a salty spring, strong on the tongue,
which is the highest attribute of man:
by that wild spirit he endures his fate,

subversive, consequential, unheroic,
as common as thistles in a cowfield.
Consider these old men, whose good old cause
was a lost cause, and in Lord Strafford's hall
black hangings rotted for two hundred years:
Milton died alone in his terraced house
outside the walls among Moorfield plague pits,
where London crumbled into sooty meadow,
where the *fanatics* died and were buried,
whose Bibles told them Cromwell comes again,
who saw the prophets hanged in Coleman Street
and Satan perching on the dome of Paul's:
are they not the forefathers of our lives?
Who paid more heed to poets than Angus
who better traced by price and date and style
all the cavortings of the British muse.
Milton in poetry renewed Eden,
the garden gone now, and the nakedness
of human passion shivering in the leaves,
in his mind, in his life, he renewed them.
What flowered then, what was it flowered and fell
in Tennyson, so wild and so untamed,
young Tennyson and in that aged man
roaring with rage in the gravels of his voice,
old Tennyson, the light in his wild eyes?
Who knew but our historian of the Whigs
in his wildness and his sobriety?
And all that knowledge turned to nothing else
but pure delight, that dropped a tear or two
over that poetry, that humanity.
Somewhere in him there was an antiquary
crabbed and beaming and from an earlier age,
drawn by that smell of cloves that lives in books:
fuel for the historian's boilers.
They tell us nothing lives but the useful,

there was that in Angus argues otherwise:
from this most useful life spread like a tree,
like a great tree beside running water.

VI

How flat it is suddenly and how still
now that the sun has wandered off the hill
and the last shadows of a sunbeam comb
the cowherds and the cattle drifting home:
it is always this moment of memory,
midsummer's broken down machinery
ruined under the first star of autumn,
and the chronometer set to kingdom come.
We are all under Samuel Palmer's spell:
when lovely Eve and trembling Adam fell
letting loose Eros, they let loose passion
to shake the mind and all that it feeds on.
The colour of daylight dissolves and fades,
a last bird twitters in the echoing shades
with no comfort for anyone but the dead:
like fainting canvas, like something painted.

Conversation with Philip Sherrard

I

The olive grove is lying still in jars,
and the eye shivers in the furthest stars:
after the summer's spice and trumpet blast
these giant moons will shatter the whole year
and now our visions will transform to fear:
shallows, sun-shadows and ground-mist at last.

II

A withering the ear cannot detect
groans in verse, poetry is too perfect,
we are old, and our children and their song
fade like heroes and heroines of the stage
hundreds of years ago, to rise in rage;
this cave of stone will not last very long.

III

It is the spirit breaks into our lives
swarming like bees from honey and their hives,
who knows from what deep nook, dark treasuries?
So Dante: you that have health of intellect
consider what is here hidden, and detect
mere poetry, her deeper mysteries.

IV

These heavy moons come trundling between cloud,
the mountain glowers and the wind is loud,
a hungry horn howling for ghostly deer:
combing the valley and the untrodden path
where the cold mountain takes her midnight bath,
fantasy of the dying mountaineer.

V

The sway of stems, the lilac-shaded glow
of our white opium-poppies come and go,
rooted in rough sand on a gravel spit
where the Court lake's black water overflows
and broken oars rot in the coarse shallows,
strayed from the wind or birds that swim on it.

VI

Yet year by year we are visited by them,
the blue-white flower-heads cool on the tall stem,
now here, now there, in the heat of July:
the aspen darkening to black as sin
flings down a shadow like a tarpaulin
and ragged tops of trees look starved and dry.

VII

This is unnatural, it will not last,
it is some weather dreamed up from the past
when the tanned shepherd feared the blue wood-smoke
while the gross bulk of his enormous sheep
lay down to pant, or heaved their sides in sleep,
and honey dripped down the God-hollowed oak.

VIII

The old themes of poetry have run sour,
the yellow silk river, the sunset hour
have curdled, the gnat whines over the stream
and the child paddling after stickleback
in the bored twilight never looking back
transforms into a ghost haunting a dream.

IX

How limited the world is and how light,
how long in moon-led dazes of delight
we threaded cadences to our sublime,
urging the singing lines of muses on
with no idea of what they smiled upon,
and not a thought those days were our good time.

X

Life rolled like landscape to the perfect west,
mountain-crest beyond glimmering mountain-crest,
and then the whole world crumbled round our heads,
you could no longer hear the waterfall,
seasons came too late for the old bird-call,
the sweating nightmares lay between our beds.

XI

I am a thing of bone that cannot sing,
there is no lingering music in the string.
I am accustomed to the peacock wail,
not to dawn chorus or the night service
that quiets all the woods to paradise
and the long echoes of the nightingale,

XII

that still laments and musically calls
as silence into deeper silence falls,
and the moon peers down like a shelly stone
into the mossy parts of the forest
where the dim stars rape all they sway to rest,
while the self-echoing bird sings on alone.

XIII

With eyes as dim as star-choirs what I see
is mere apology for poetry:
daylight is stony, twilight stellifies,
I see wonders: sixty years I saw none,
now fresh from dreaming they rise like a sun
to burn the gauzy curtains from my eyes.

XIV

It is written I am still to sing like him,
blind poet of Sion and Sion's hymn
who in his darkness like the nightingale
made an unearthly music in his house,
in his small house whose spirit might arouse
sleek angels of a God that would not fail.

XV

Philip, they are talking about the dead.
How all these things come fizzing through the head:
how inexpressible and curious
that all the gods of Greece, the archaic myth,
utterly die, what we continue with
is the golden-lipped angels of Solomos.

XVI

Liberty of the heroes, cool with no sound
scything the wicket at Lord's cricket ground,
the angel of poor canvas, Victory,
the one Byzantine truly magical
and truly mythic real among them all:
power of salt and silver and the sea.

XVII

Byzantine angel, Philip, wine that ran
in Byron's veins because he was a man,
loved what we loved and feared the things we feared,
Solomos hunted it and heard it run
in blind men outside wine-shops in the sun,
and runs now down your face, in your white beard.

XVIII

Philip, you are not framed in the sunlight
but some pure crumb of fire kindled in it,
deep in the sun passion rehearses death
and worthy of that spring of holy fires
sober from poetry, that which conspires
and is the ash of God and of his breath.

XIX

The words rasp in my throat, and poetry
like poisonous sea-water cries in me
brute music and dark glitter of the sea-swell
and the sun's shadow stricken by the sun:
shadow by shadow falls, never undone
only remade, like Eliot's shore-bell.

XX

The thin bell jangling in the water's throat
heard by the dying sailor from his boat,
tone the mist baffles and the waves confuse,
no comfort from sunbreathings or moonsighs:
moondazzles and sunfire consume the eyes,
the bell dangles and jangles like the music.

XXI

It is the season now for poetry
when the hard sun creeps into the still sky
flooding the long hill-tops in yellow heat,
painting the plains greenest of inland things,
to wake the night-wet bird from shiverings:
but the bird is still and dead that sang so sweet.

XXII

Poetry fades as the bee vanishes,
hard-working as a woman, yet she sees
eight suns and when the garden cools she knows,
the ruins are deserted, and at last
the entire season of poetry is past,
the expiring piddle of a garden hose.

XXIII

The cave-wall, dank and streaming as a fish-skin
where the wave booms sucking the echoes in
will crumble as you scratch it with your hand,
green grey to charcoal to a sand of blue,
and everything that the sea says is true,
the sea's rough whisper will not rest in sand.

XXIV

This sand of stars that quivers in the sky
lapping dark water like dogs as they die
howls with hunger nothing on earth can fill,
the light is lessening, star dwindles to bone,
the cold star-ashes shiver into stone,
thousands of years let them sleep and lie still.

The Graveyard by the Sea

FROM PAUL VALÉRY

I

That quiet roof, promenade of pigeons,
Quivers between pine trees, between tomb-stones.
Midday justice creates a sea of fire,
The sea begins again, again, again,
Rewards for meditation and its pain
In that long calmness that the gods inspire:

II

What pure labour, consumed into fine light,
Vast diamond of foam too fine for sight,
And what a peace it is that we feel grow,
When sun rests on the abyss and seems to pause,
Pure construct of an everlasting cause:
Time is a glitter and the Dream to know.

III

Stable treasure, Athene's simple shrine,
Mass of calm, white reserve that can be seen,
Fastidious water, Eye in which one feels
So much of sleep under a veil of flame,
O my silence, soul-building or soul-game,
Roof, slope of gold made of a thousand tiles!

IV

Defined by just one sigh, temple of Time:
Grown used to you, to this pure point I climb,
Surrounded by horizons of sea light:
And as to gods my supreme offering,
Nothing is sown from that still glittering
But absolute contempt in the sky's height.

V

As the fruit fuses dying into pleasure
And ruining turns to delight so pure
That in the mouth of joy the fruit-form dies,
I bury here the fires that shall have fumed:
Heaven sings to the soul that is consumed
River-murmurs, re-echoes of ferries.

VI

Fine heaven, true heaven, see how I change
After so much of pride, so much of strange
Idleness, and yet full of power I face
Abandonment to the void brilliance,
Over the dwellings of the dead I advance,
My shadow tamed to its weak, ghostly pace.

VII

My soul has passed the flames of the solstice
And I uphold that admirable justice
Of light, in arms that pitilessly glow!
I give you the first place and the pure height:
See what you are!... And yet to reflect light
Supposes a dark side made of shadow.

VIII

For me alone to me alone in me
Close to the heart the springs of poetry,
In between emptiness and pure and dumb
I wait on the echo of greatness within,
Bitter cistern, sombre and deep-sounding
Soul-echo of a hollow, always to come.

IX

Do you know, phoney captive of foliage,
Gulf, eater away of this thin iron cage,
Eyes shut, the secrets dazzling in my head,
What body drags me to its lazy end,
What brow draws it to this old bony ground?
A spark of light is thinking of my dead.

X

Enclosed, sacred, full of fire without weight
Earthly fragment offered up to the light,
This place pleases me overlorded by flames,
Made of gold and of sombre trees and stones
Where so much marble shivers under dark tones,
The faithful sea is sleeping on my tombs!

XI

My gleaming bitch, keep off idolatry,
When with a shepherd's smile alone I see
Them grazing long, white sheep of mystery,
And guarded white herd of my tranquil tombs
Drive far away from them the clever pigeons,
Vain dreams, angelic curiosity.

XII

Now that it's here, the future is lazy,
The tidy insect scrapes where ground is dry,
All is burned and unmade, consumed in air
To who knows what severe essential spirit,
Life is immense, it is drunken with death,
And bitterness is sweet, spirit is clear.

XIII

The hidden dead lie in earth easily,
It warms them and dries out their mystery.
Midday overhead, a Noon without moving
Thinks himself in himself as befits him,
The complete head and perfect diadem,
In you I am the element altering.

XIV

For all your fears you have no one but me!
Remorse and doubt and failure work in me:
They are the flaw in the great diamond...
But in this massive night of heavy stone,
In the tree-roots a people scarcely seen
Move slowly to your side as if summoned.

XV

They have fused into a fog of non-being,
Red clay has drunk beauty's white blossoming,
The gift of living passes to green leaf!
Where are the dead with their familiar phrase
Their personal art, their souls' particular ways?
Maggots go by where the tears grew from grief.

XVI

And those sharp cries of girls tickled at play
The eyes, the teeth, the wet lids of the eye,
The charming breast that plays at the fire-game,
The blood bright in the lips as they surrender
The final gifts, fingers their last defender,
All go to earth and back into the game.

XVII

And you great soul, do you hope for a dream
Without these colourings that merely seem,
That waves and gold create in bodily eyes?
When you are turned to vapour will you sing?
All disappears, I am no solid thing,
And the divine impatience also dies.

XVIII

Thin immortality, black and gilded,
Consoler with the terrible laurelled head,
And death a mother's breast for which we feel,
The noble lie, and the religious ruse,
Who does not know them, who would not refuse
That empty skull and that eternal smile?

XIX

O deep fathers, head-bones that are still full
Under the weight of many a shovelfull,
You are the earth, you muffled our footfall:
True consumer, the worm that burrows deep
Waits not for you who below stones sleep,
He lives on life, his bite's perpetual.

XX

Love maybe, or self-hatred should it be?
His secret biting is so close to me,
There is no name that is not fit for him!
Who cares? He wishes, touches, sees, and dreams,
He loves my flesh, and even in bed it seems
I live by him, dependent as a limb.

XXI

Zeno! Elean Zeno, cruel Zeno,
You have pierced me with that feathered arrow
That quivers, yet it flies and does not fly,
The sound my father but the arrow death,
Ah sun... the tortoise shadow soul and breath,
Still Achilles, mere immobility.

XXII

No, no... Upright! For all futurity
Break up this meditative form, body!
The wind is born, my heart, drink and revive!
There is a freshness breathing from the sea
Restores my soul... O salted potency!
Run at the waves and then recoil alive!

XXIII

Yes! Mighty sea rich with delirium
In panther-skin and in torn chlamys, from
A thousand thousand images of the sun
Absolved, O Hydra, drunk on your blue flesh,
Biting your own tail's golden sparkling mesh,
Your tumult and your silence are all one.

XXIV

The wind rises... life calls for a new fling,
The infinite air has my page fluttering,
Waves break and grind to powder on mere stone,
Bewildered pages fly like foam away,
Break up waves rejoicing, and sweep away
This quiet roof where yachts peck up and down.